Do You Not See 連理樹

HARPER COLOPHON BOOKS
Harper & Row, Publishers
New York, Cambridge, Hagerstown, Philadelphia, San Francisco
London, Mexico City, São Paulo, Sydney

Edited and adapted by Sally F. Nichols

Grateful acknowledgement is made to the following publishers and translators for permission to reprint:

George Allen & Unwin for "Planting Flowers on the Eastern Embankment" by Po Chü-i from *More Translations from the Chinese*.

Columbia University Press for an excerpt from the description of the Shang-lin Park of the Son of Heaven by Ssu-ma Hsiang-ju from *Early Chinese Literature* and "Lament of the Farm Wife of Wu" from *Su Tung-p'o: Selections from a Sung Dynasty Poet*.

Constable & Company, Ltd. for "Song of the White Clouds" from *Lyrics from the Chinese*.

Grove Press for "The Soldier's Song" and "Song of Courtship" from *The Book of Songs*. Reprinted by permission of Grove Press, Inc. First Grove Press edition 1960.

Harvard University Press for "Drought" from *Shih-Ching: The Classic Anthology Defined by Confucius*, Ezra Pound, editor and translator. Copyright © 1959 by the President and Fellows of Harvard College.

David Hawkes, translator, for an excerpt from "Li Sao" from *Ch'u Tzu: The Songs of the South, An Ancient Chinese Anthology*.

Lund Humphries Publishers, Ltd. for "Poems of My Heart (5)" by Juan Chi from *Poems of Solitude*.

Alfred A. Knopf, Inc. for "Planting Flowers on the Eastern Embankment" by Po Chü-i from *Translations from the Chinese*, translated by Arthur Waley. Copyright 1919 and renewed 1947 by Arthur Waley. Reprinted by permission of Alfred A. Knopf, Inc.

New Directions for "South Wind" by Tu Fu from *One Hundred Poems from the Chinese*. Copyright © 1971 by Kenneth Rexroth, "To the Tune 'Spring of Wu Ling'" by Li Ch'ing-chao from *Love and the Turning Year: One Hundred More Poems from the Chinese*. Copyright © 1970 by Kenneth Rexroth. All rights reserved. Reprinted by permission of New Directions.

Paragon Book Reprint Corp. for "A Summer Day" by Li Po from *Works of Li Po, The Chinese Poet*.

Stanford University Press for "To Him I Love" by Tzu Yeh and "Wise Age to Youth" by Tu Ch'iu-niang from *Poems of the Hundred Names*.

Charles E. Tuttle Co., Inc. for "At Wei River Farm" and "Light Verse on a Rock" from *Poems by Wang Wei*.

This work is an adaptation of the limited-edition portfolio published by The Truax Press, Inc.

Readings of the two English translations and in Mandarin (presented in this edition) are separately available. For information address The Truax Press, Inc., P.O. Box 157, Skiff Mountain Road, Kent, Connecticut 06757.

First HARPER COLOPHON edition published 1980.

LIBRARY OF CONGRESS CATALOG CARD NUMBER: 79-3833

ISBN: 0-06-090772-X

80 81 82 83 84 10 9 8 7 6 5 4 3 2 1

Contents

Acknowledgments

With great pleasure I acknowledge my indebtedness and gratitude to those who have given me of their insights, knowledge and kindness. There have been many, but most particularly I would like to thank: Mr. Howard Rovics, composer; Prof. James J. Y. Liu, Department of Asian Languages, Stanford University; Prof. Burton D. Watson, Department of East Asian Languages, Columbia University; Mrs. Barbara Blitzer, Director, Creative Services, Macmillan Publishing Co.; Miss Loretta Pan, who not only contributed the calligraphy but whose critical opinion has been invaluable; John Hickman Phillips, Ph.D.; and my husband, Elliott S. Nichols.

Although there are many limitations inherent in the nature of a multi-levelled approach to poetry and in the proferred effort, the inadvertent ones are my own.

SALLY F. NICHOLS

Foreword

Anyone who has written his own poetry, tried to translate someone else's or simply read poetry with attention and thoughtfulness, has at some time no doubt asked himself the question: Just where does the poem exist? If he is a writer of poetry, he is only too familiar with that luminous cloud that hovers tauntingly over his head when he is in the midst of composition, casting fleet shadows across his brain but remaining always just out of reach. This is the poem he hoped to write, the poem that in the end got away, the poem that will never be written.

In its place he has these earnest markings on the page, the contour of the poem captured. He himself knows what relation these notations bear to the commotion that attacked him. But can anyone else decipher his marks accurately and reconstruct from them the same stir and excitement? Does the poem in fact no longer exist in the mind of its maker, but now has its being in pencil or brush strokes, typescript or printed text alone?

No—the letters and punctuation marks are surely no more than a form of rough notation, a score to guide the artist who will create the music and life of the poem from the silent symbols on the page. The poem must reside, then, not in the logographic conventions that figure it on paper, but in the voice and imagination of the reader, the intoner, who functions as its new creator. But if this is so, it follows that there must be as many different poems as there are readers. . . . At this point, one shrinks from pursuing the train of thought further, fearful of where it may lead.

For the translator, such reflections can be even more complex and disquieting. He must inquire not only what is the genesis of the original poem, where it exists and by what process it has come into his possession, but what relation his own recreation of it in another language bears to the original, where this new poem of his in turn exists, and what proportion of it faithfully reflects the original, what proportion his own opaque and interposing self. How successfully, for example, have sense and mood survived the precarious passage from one language to another; what echoes, if any, remain of the former music; have the imagery, the calligraphic effect, the vibrance in any appreciable degree been borne over?

Do You Not See, the work which it is my pleasure to introduce here, attempts to grapple with these problems through a unique assemblage of materials, which are divided into two parts. The core of Part One is a series of poems in English—translations of poems or parts of poems written in classical Chinese. So that the reader may respond most fully to their aesthetic qualities, the English translations are presented in attractive lettered form. The poems are paired with the remarkable pen drawings of Sally Nichols—renderings of natural scenes that in their tensile tracery recall the calligraphic impact of the English poems, which in turn echoes the still more potent calligraphy of the Chinese originals. The poems are also presented in the original Chinese. The handwritten calligraphy allows the reader to appreciate the visual impact of each poem in something like the form in which it came from its creator's brush.

Part Two, in order to try to make as clear as possible just what has been involved in the translation process in each case, offers a literal translation of each poem and a structural analysis to show just how its form and syntax function.

With these materials at hand to manipulate at will, the reader is in a position to savor the English poem, to ponder the Chinese original from which it in some sense derives, and to gauge the nature and degree of that derivation. The apparatus, moreover, enables the reader not only to move backward to the aesthetic antecedents of the English poems but to venture forward on at least one stage of a new artistic journey, set in motion by the poems, through the drawings that accompany them.

Thus the play of visual forces is carried forward—the intricate dance of artistic impulse and response given freedom to progress through yet another figure. These materials enable the reader to follow each phase and modulation of the dance, and, if so inspired, to lead it through some wholly new progression of his own devising.

It is a highly unusual collection, compiled with great care and imagination, a novel attempt to probe into the life of poems and their translations, to reveal their mechanisms, and to suggest some of the ways in which their vitality surmounts boundaries of language and medium and expands constantly outward.

BURTON WATSON

PART ONE

The Poems

1. "South Wind" by Tu Fu, translated by Kenneth Rexroth

南風

杜甫

遲日江山麗
春風花草香
泥融飛燕子
沙暖睡鴛鴦

The days grow long, the mountains beautiful.
The south wind blows
Over blossoming meadows.
Newly arrived swallows dart
Over steaming marshes.
Ducks in pairs drowse on the warm sand.

2. "Planting flowers on the Eastern Embankment" by Po Chü-I, translated by Arthur Waley

东坡種花

白居易

持钱买花樹
城东坡上栽
但購有花者
不限桃杏梅
百果参雜種
千枝次第開
天时有早晚
地力有高低
红者霞艷々
白者雪皚々
遊蜂逐不去
好鳥亦来栖
前有長流水
下有小平台
时拂台上石
一舉風前杯
花枝蔭我頭
花蕊落我懷
独酌復独詠
不覺日平西
巴俗不愛花
竟春無人来
唯此醉太守
盡日不能迴

I took money and bought flowering trees
And planted them out on the bank to the east of the Keep.
I simply bought whatever had most blooms,
Not caring whether peach, apricot, or plum.
A hundred fruits, all mixed up together;
A thousand branches, flowering in due rotation.
Each has its season coming early or late;
But to all alike the fertile soil is kind.
The red flowers gleam like a fall of snow.
The wandering bees cannot bear to leave them;
The sweet birds also come there to roost.
In front there flows an ever-running stream;
Beneath there is built a little flat terrace;
Sometimes I sweep the flagstones of the terrace;
Sometimes, in the wind, I raise my cup and drink.
The flower-branches screen my head from the sun;
The flower-buds fall down into my lap.
Alone drinking, alone singing my songs
I do not notice that the moon is level with the steps.
The people of Pa do not care for flowers;
All spring no one has come to look.
But their Governor General, alone with his cup of wine,
Sits till evening and will not move from the place!

3. "Songs of Courtship" from *The Book of Songs* translated by Arthur Waley

野有蔓草　诗经

野有蔓草　零露漙兮

有美一人　清揚婉兮

邂逅相遇　適我願兮

野有蔓草　零露瀼々

有美一人　婉如清揚

邂逅相遇　与子偕臧

Out in the bushlands a creeper grows,
The falling dew lies thick upon it.
There was a man so lovely,
Clear-brow well rounded.
By chance I came across him,
And he let me have my will.

Out in the bushlands a creeper grows,
The falling dew lies heavy on it.
There was a man so lovely,
Well rounded his clear brow.
By chance I came upon him:
"Oh, Sir, to be with you is good."

4. "A Summer Day" by Li Po, translated by Shigeyoshi Obata

山间夏日　李白

嬾搖白羽扇
躶体青林中
脫巾挂石壁
露頂洒松風

Naked I lie in the green forest of summer . . .
Too lazy to wave my white feathered fan.
I hang my hat on a crag,
And bare my head to the wind that comes
Blowing through the pine trees.

5. "The Soldier's Song" from The Book of Songs translated by Arthur Waley

何草不黃

詩經

何草不黃　何日不行
何人不將　經營四方
何草不玄　何人不矜
哀我征夫　獨為匪民
匪兕匪虎　率彼曠野
哀我征夫　朝夕不暇
有芃者狐　率彼幽草
有棧之車　行彼周道

What plant is not faded?
What day we do not march?
What man is not taken
To defend the four bounds?

What plant is not wilting?
What man is not taken from his wife?
Alas for us soldiers,
Treated as though we were not fellow-men!

Are we buffaloes, are we tigers
That our home should be these
desolate wilds?
Alas for us soldiers,
Neither by day nor night can we rest!

The fox bumps and drags
Through the tall thick grass.
Inch by inch move our barrows
As we push them along the track.

6. "To Him I Love" by Tzu Yeh, translated by Henry H. Hart

贈愛

女子子夜

欢愁儂亦慘
郎笑我便喜
不見連理樹
异根同條起

Do you not see
That you and I
Are as the branches
Of one tree?
With your rejoicing
Comes my laughter;
With your sadness
Start my tears.
Love,
Could life be otherwise
With you and me?

7. "At Wei River farm" by Wang Wei, translated by Chang Yin-nan and Lewis C. Walmsley

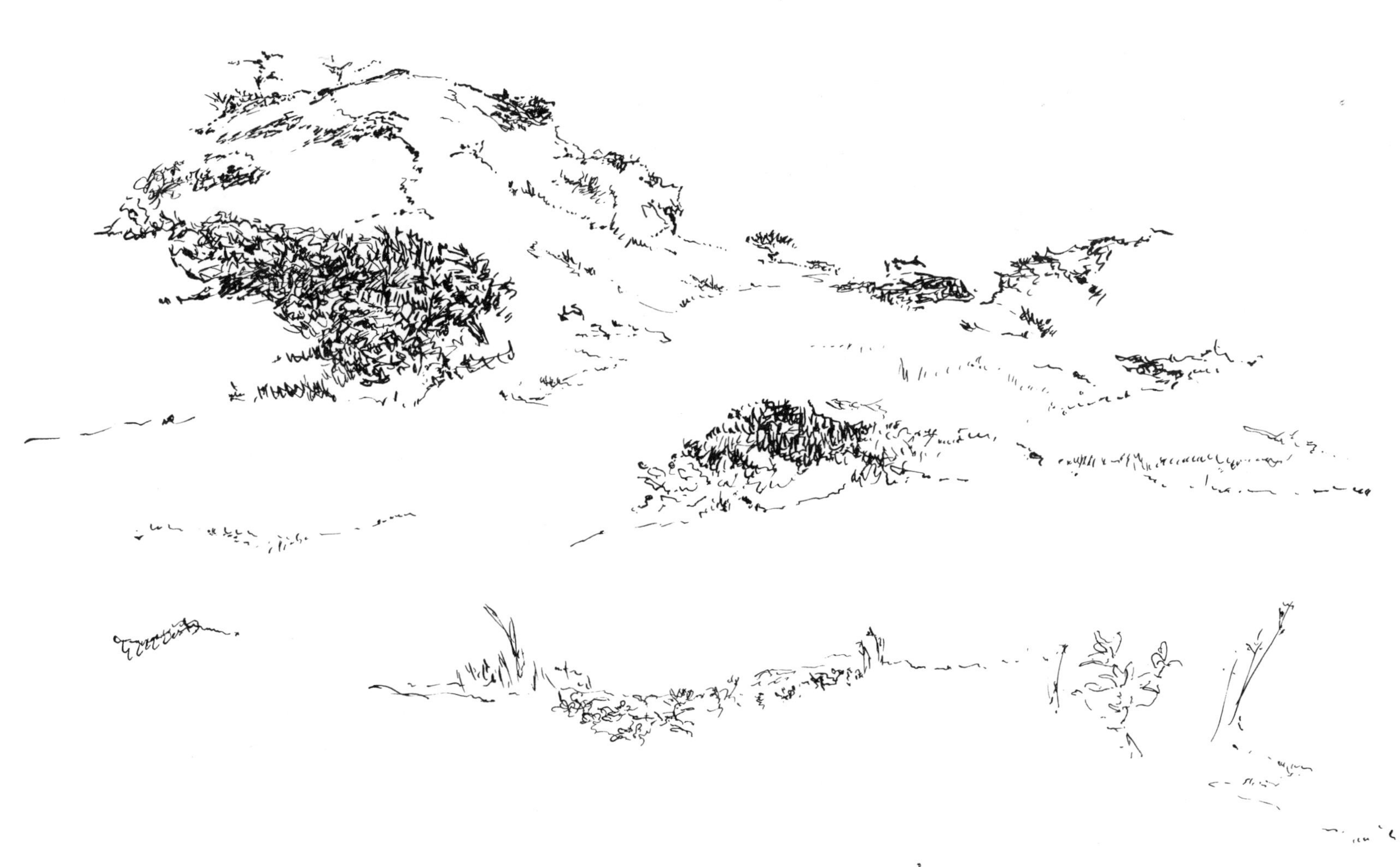

渭川田家　王維

斜光照墟落
窮巷牛羊归
野老念牧童
倚杖候荊扉
雉雊麥苗秀
蚕眠桑葉稀
田夫荷鋤立
相見語依々
即此羨閑逸
悵然歌式微

Reluctant night spreads lingering twilight
across the forgotten village;
Cattle and sheep wind homeward
through the narrow lanes.
Leaning heavily on his staff, the old peasant
waits beside his thatched door;
He worries over his tardy shepherd son...
Strutting pheasants call in the rich young wheat fields;
Silkworms slumber;
few mulberry leaves remain.
Hoes slung across shoulders,
farmers clump along home,
And meeting their fellows, loiter to chatter incessantly...
I long for their leisure and sense of ease!
I try to hide my envy by humming the old song of Shih-wei!

8. "Song of the White Clouds" from an ancient source, translated by Helen Waddell

白雲謠

白雲在天
丘陵自出
道里悠遠
山川间之
將子無死
尚復能來

White clouds are in the sky.
    Great shoulders of the hills
Between us two must lie.
    The road is rough and far.
Deep fords between us are.
    I pray you not to die.

9. "Wise Age to Youth" by Tu Ch'iu-niang, translated by Henry H. Hart

金縷衣

杜秋娘

勸君莫惜金縷衣
勸君須惜少年時
花開堪折直須折
莫待無花空折枝

Wear your gold and silken garments;
Store not one of them away;
Flaunt them in your years of beauty
Ere the world grows old and gray.

Pluck the blossoms in the springtime
When they open to the sun,
For you'll find but withered branches
When bright youth and love are done.

10. "Poems of My Heart (5)" by Juan Chi, translated by Jerome Ch'en and Michael Bullock

詠懷詩

阮籍

開秋兆涼風
蟋蟀鳴牀帷
感物懷殷憂
悄々令心悲
多言焉所告
繁辭將訴誰
微風吹罗袂
明月耀清暉
晨鸡鳴高樹
命駕起旋归

Autumn is beginning,
the weather is turning chill.
Crickets move in to sing under my bed.
A thousand things surge into my mind
And grieve my heart.
A thousand tales search for words;
But to whom will they be told?
The morning breeze flows under my sleeves,
The moonlight thins,
And the cock crows,
As I turn my horses' heads
towards home.

11. Excerpt from the description of the Shang-lin Park of the Son of Heaven

by Ssu-ma Hsiang-ju, translated by Burton Watson

上林賦

司馬相如

於是乎崇山矗々巃嵸崔巍
深林巨木嶄巖參差九嵕巀嶭
南山峩々巖陁甗錡摧崣崛崎
振溪通谷蹇產溝瀆谽呀豁閜
阜陵別隝崴磈㟪廆丘虛堀礨
隱轔鬱壘登降施靡陂池貏豸
沇溶淫鬻散渙夷陸亭皋千里
靡不被築揜以綠蕙被以江蘺
糅以蘼蕪雜以留夷布結縷
攢戾莎揭車衡蘭槀本射干
茈薑蘘荷葴持若蓀鮮支黃礫
蔣芧青薠布濩閎澤延曼太原
麗靡廣衍應風披靡吐芳揚烈
郁々菲々衆香發越肸蠁布寫
晻薆咇茀

Behind them rise the tall mountains,
Lofty crests lifted to the sky;
Clothed in dense forests of giant trees,
Jagged with peaks and crags;
The steep summits of the Nine Pikes,
The towering heights of the Southern Mountains,
Soar dizzily like a stack of cooking pots,
Precipitous and sheer.
Their sides are furrowed with ravines and valleys,
Narrow-mouthed clefts and open glens,
Through which rivulets dart and wind.
About their base, hills and islands
Raise their tall heads;
Ragged knolls and hillocks
Rise and fall,
Twisting and twining
Like the coiled bodies of reptiles;
While from their folds the mountain streams
leap and tumble,
Spilling out upon the level plains.
There they flow a thousand miles
along smooth beds,
Their banks lined with dikes
Blanketed with green orchids
And hidden beneath selinea,
Mingled with snakemouth
And magnolias;
Planted with yucca,
Sedge of purple dye,
Bittersweet, gentians, and orchis,
Blue flag and crow-fans,
Ginger and turmeric,
Monkshood, wolfbane,
Nightshade, basil,
Mint, ramie, and blue artemisia,
Spreading across the wide swamps,
Rambling over the broad plains,
A vast and unbroken mass of flowers,
Nodding before the wind;
Breathing their fragrance,
Pungent and sweet,
A hundred perfumes
Wafted abroad
Upon the scented air.

12. "Lament of the Farm Wife of Wu" by Su Tung-p'o, translated by Burton Watson

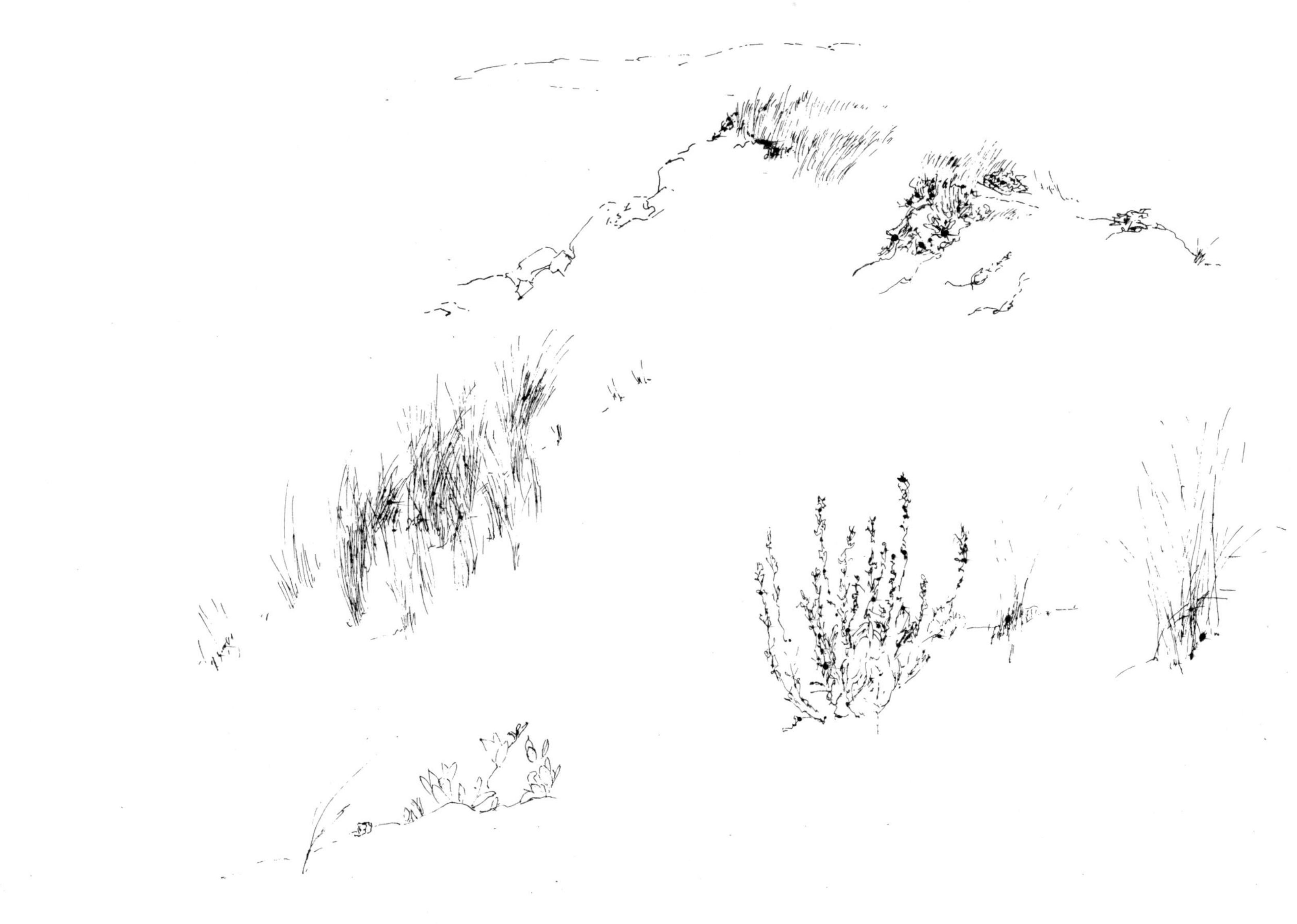

吳中田婦歎

苏东坡

今年粳稻熟苦遲
庶見霜風来幾時
風霜来时雨如瀉
把頭出菌鐮生衣
眼枯淚盡雨不盡
忍見黃穗臥青泥
茅苫一月隴上宿
天晴穫稻隨車歸
汗流肩赬載入市
價賤乞與如糠粞
賣牛納稅拆屋炊
慮淺不及明年飢
官今要錢不要米
西北万里招羌兒
龔黃滿朝人更苦
不如却作河伯婦

Rice this year ripens so late!
We watch, but when will the frost winds come?
They come - with rain in bucketfuls;
The harrow sprouts mold, the sickle rusts.
    My tears are all cried out, but rain never ends;
    It hurts to see yellow stalks flattened in the mud.
We camped in a grass shelter a month by the fields;
Then it cleared and we reaped the grain,
followed the wagon home,
Sweaty shoulders sore, carting it to town -
The price it fetched, you'd think we came with chaff.
We sold the ox to pay for taxes,
Broke up the roof for kindling;
We'll get by for a time, but what of next year's hunger?
    Officials demand cash now - they won't take grain;
    The long northwest border tempts invaders.
Wise men fill the court - why do things get worse?
I'd be better off bride to the River Lord!

13. "To the Tune 'Spring of Wu Ling'" by Li Ch'ing-chao, translated by Kenneth Rexroth

武陵春

李清照

風住塵香花已盡
日晚倦梳頭
物是人非事々休
欲語淚先流
聞說双溪春尚好
也擬泛輕舟
只恐双溪舴艋舟
載不動許多愁

The gentle breeze has died down.
The perfumed dust has settled.
It is the end of the time
Of flowers. Evening falls
And all day I have been too
Lazy to comb my hair.
The toilet articles are there,
But the man is gone away.
All effort would be wasted.
When I try to sing, my tears
Choke me, I dreamed my flower boat
Carried me to him, but I
Know so fragile a vessel
Won't bear such a weight of sorrow.

14. "Drought" from The Confucian Odes translated by Ezra Pound

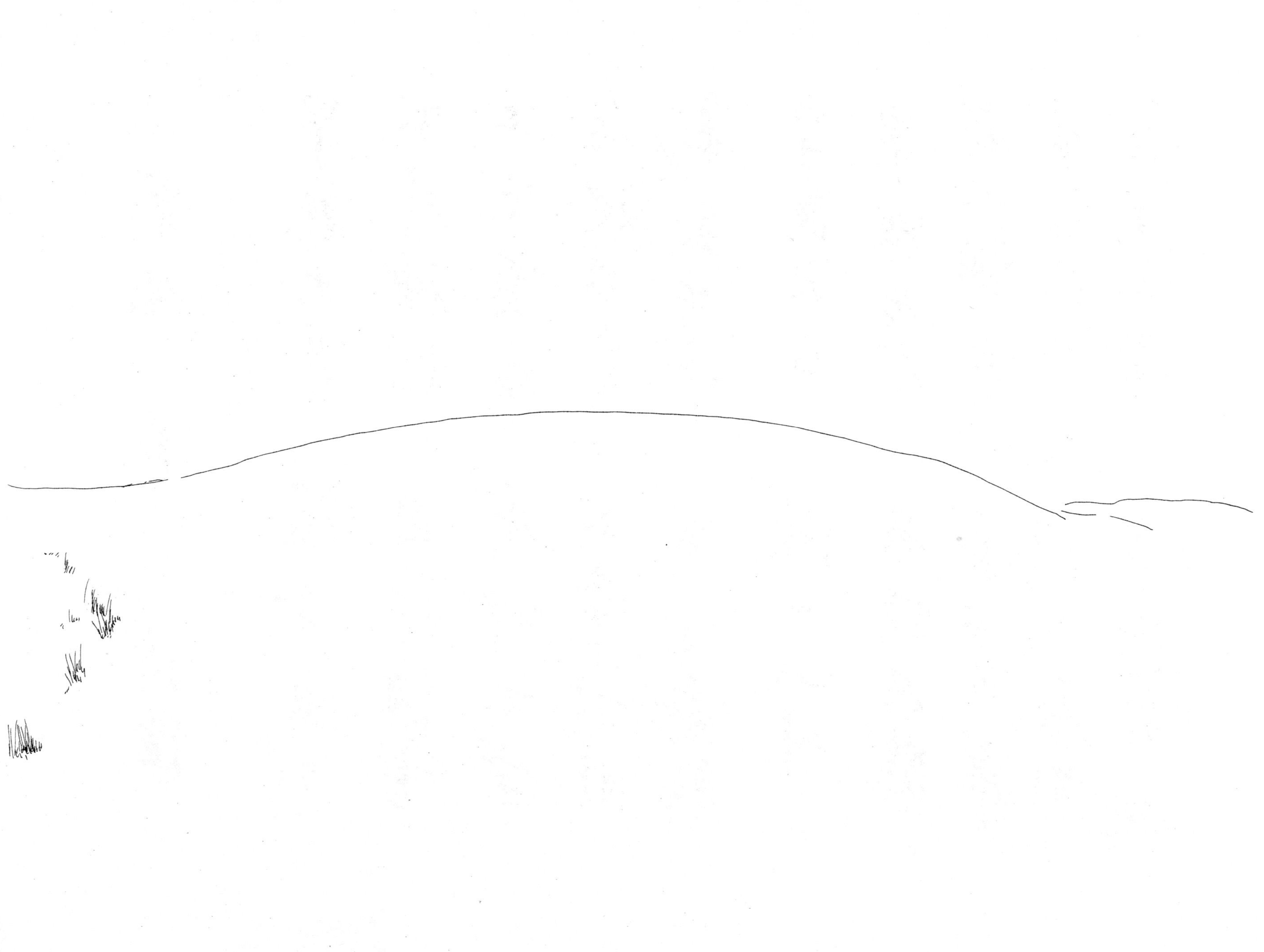

旱既大甚

詩经

旱既大甚　蘊隆虫々
不殄禋祀　自郊徂宫
上下奠瘞　靡神不宗
后稷不克　上帝不臨
耗斁下土　寧丁我躬
旱既大甚　滌々山川
旱魃为虐　如惔如焚
我心憚暑　憂心如熏
羣公先正　则不我聞
昊天上帝　寧俾我遯

The great drought is come as parching,
Quilted with locusts and swollen,
There is no sacrifice I have not offered
Neither have I neglected the bournes nor their altars,
Above, below, I have offered up offering
And I have buried.
There is no power I have not honoured,
The Lord Tsi does not uphold us
Nor the power of heaven approach us,
Waste, devast the earth,
Would that it fell upon me, on my person only!

Great the drought, the high hills are parched
And their rivers withered away,
Without and within the fire-demons consume us,
My heart is made barren with the sorrow of burning,
The pastoral dukes of aforetime will not hear us
Neither will the bright god over heaven
Permit me to lay down my charge.

15. from "Li Sao", attributed to Ch'u Yüan, translated by David Hawkes

離騷

屈原

朝發軔於蒼梧兮
　夕余至乎縣圃
欲少留此灵瑣兮
　日忽忽其將暮
吾令羲和弭節兮
　望崦嵫而勿迫
路曼曼其脩遠兮
　吾將上下而求索

吾令凤鳥飛騰兮
　继之以日夜
飄風屯其相離兮
　帥雲霓而來御
紛總總其離合兮
　斑陸離其上下
吾令帝閽開關兮
　倚閶闔而望予

In the morning I started on my way from Ts'ang-wu
    In the evening I came to the Garden of Paradise.
I wanted to stay a while in those fairy precincts,
    But the swift-moving sun was dipping to the west.
I ordered Hsi-ho to stay the sun steeds gallop,
    To stand over Yen-tzu mountain and not go in.
Long, long had been my road and far, far was the journey:
    I would go up and down to seek my heart's desire.

I caused my phoenixes to mount on their pinions
    And fly ever onward by night and by day.
The whirlwinds gathered and came out to meet me,
    Leading clouds and rainbows, to give me welcome.
In wild confusion, now joined and now parted,
    Upwards and downwards rushed the glittering train.
I asked Heaven's porter to open up for me;
    But he leant across Heaven's gate and eyed me churlishly.

16. "Light Verse on a Rock" by Wang Wei, translated by Chang Yin-nan and Lewis C. Walmsley

戲題磐石　王維

可憐磐石臨泉水
復有垂楊拂酒盃
若道春風不解意
何因吹送落花來

I pity the inert rock by the flowing stream
And the willows trailing fingers into my wine-cup...
But who can say the spring wind is not aware
of the sound in my heart?
Why else should it blow these frail falling petals about me?

PART TWO

Translations and Analyses

by Stuart H. Sargent

Introduction

The fact that the poems which inspired this multi-leveled production are translations from a foreign tongue suggests still another level which many may wish to see explored: namely, the beauty of the poems in the original Chinese. In spite of the linguistic barrier which keeps this beauty from most of us, there are ways to enable the interested Western reader to at least begin to get a feeling for what a Chinese poem is really like. I have used "literal," word-for-word translations, romanized transcriptions, and metric patterns to this end. The Chinese texts also appear in printed form. Whether the reader goes through this material carefully, or simply gives it a casual glance, I hope it will add another dimension to his experience of these Chinese poems.

The translations are not offered as an example of how I think poetry should, in general, be translated, for though there may be a certain power to some of the lines, the cramming of English words into foreign syntax leads too easily to incomprehensibility or, worse, miscomprehension, and leaves few resources other than vocabulary with which to try to recreate the rich polyphony of the original poem. Still, having such word-for-word versions to refer to in connection with more interpretive translations can be helpful in suggesting the conciseness of Chinese poetry and making more apparent in a given poem regularity or irregularity in line length or the presence of such features as parallelisms or reduplicated words.

For this reason, literal translations are justified here, and indeed I often risked incomprehensible literalness, since the reader will have already gotten the sense from the fuller version, although those who understand Chinese will note instances where concessions to English syntax were necessary. Other deviations from word-for-word translations were required, and should be explained. In spite of the well-known fact that words in literary Chinese are usually monosyllabic, it was inevitable that I could not always have one English word per Chinese syllable: A bisyllabic word such as *"syi-shwai",* for example, became the single word "cricket"; where, on the other hand, more than one English word was required to do the work of one Chinese syllable, I joined the English words with a hyphen (*"you"* became "there-is" or "there-are," *"lwo,"* "drop," became "drop-on" when followed by "my bosom," etc.). Sometimes, too, words were added in brackets to clarify the meaning.

In Chinese poems of five- or seven-syllable lines there is a regular pause which I have marked in my translations with caesura signs. Sometimes the syntax reaches across the caesura, or suggests a secondary caesura, and sometimes the syntax and usual rhythm are mutually reinforcing. I have indicated only the basic rhythm, hoping that the reader can sense the variations as they occur.

One poem is left untranslated: "Description of the Shang-lin Park," which is an example of a type of rhyme-prose noted for long lists of flora and fauna (often with no English equivalents) and great accumulations of descriptive words which say more or less the same thing. To replace Mr. Watson's delightful variety of plants with transliterations or Latin names would certainly not bring the reader any closer to the original, nor would alternate phrasings of his "steep summits" and "towering heights" be anything but a needless thesaurus exercise.

The romanized transcriptions are for the modern Mandarin pronunciation of the words. The poems were originally pronounced differently, but although much work has been done by linguists on the reconstruction of ancient phonology, we do not know exactly how they would have sounded, and practically no one attempts to read Chinese poetry in anything but modern Chinese. (Changes from the ancient pronunciation will account for the fact that lines in these poems which do not seem to rhyme are marked as rhyming ("**r**"), and unmarked lines which look as if they end in rhymes actually did not rhyme when they were written.)

I have used the Yale system of romanization because English-speaking persons can usually begin to read it without a great deal of instruction. (Where Chinese names appear in my translations and notes, however, I follow standard practice in using the Wade-Giles system.) With the recorded readings of the poems at hand, the reader can be spared a lengthy verbal description of how to sound out this transcription.

The marks – ˊ ˇ ˋ above the words represent the four "tones" of Mandarin Chinese, the pitch contours of the word sounds which help determine the meaning of the words. Their ancient counterparts are important for understanding the "meter" of the poems, which I have represented in crosses and dashes. The dashes stand for words which were pronounced with the Level Tones, that is, with relatively long duration and little change in pitch; the crosses represent the Deflected Tones, shorter in length or changing more radically in pitch. As the Chinese became more conscious of the existence of tones in their language, they began to pay much heed to their sequence in verse, and soon specific patterns of Level and Deflected tones were fixed for certain genres in poetry. The reader can get a sense of the resulting rhythm by assigning a single-syllable name, A and B, for example, to the dashes and crosses and reading aloud. Li Po's poem would be

B A / / B B B
B B / / A A A r
B A / / B B B
B B / / B A A r

(using the Chinese names: *dze ping / / dze dze dze / / dze dze / / ping*

ping ping etc.). I have not given metric patterns for the earlier poems, as their authors were not conscious of tones—and in any case, we are not sure to what degree Chinese had become the tonal language we know in later centuries.

I have tried to keep this introduction as short and non-technical as possible, yet some readers may wish for more detailed discussion of certain aspects of Chinese poetry. An excellent source for information is *The Art of Chinese Poetry* by James J.Y. Liu (Chicago, 1962), available in paperback editions.

Finally, I wish to express my gratitude to Sally Nichols for giving me the privilege of participating in this project. She has been a wonderful person to work with, sensitive to the problems which I encountered and able to make insightful suggestions when they were most needed. My thanks also to my teachers, Professors James J.Y. Liu and Kao Kung-yi of Stanford University, to whom I turned for help with some of the knottier problems of linguistics and translation. There are, however, many details of my research which I did not verify with these experts, and I remain solely responsible for errors and infelicitous choices.

STUART H. SARGENT

1.

SOUTH WIND

Tu Fu

	Transcription of Sound		Tone Pattern	
Long day // river mountain lovely	Chŕ r̀ // jyāng shān lì		— + ‖ — — +	
Spring wind // flower grass fragrant	Chwūn fēng // hwā tsǎu syāng	r	— — ‖ — + —	r
Mud thaw // fly swallows	Ní rúng // fēi yàn dž̌		— — ‖ — + +	
Sand warm // sleep drake hen[1]	Shā nwǎn // shwèi ywān yāng	r	— + ‖ + — —	r

[1]Specifically, male and female "mandarin ducks".

南風　杜甫

遲日江山麗
春風花草香
泥融飛燕子
沙暖睡鴛鴦

2.

PLANTING FLOWERS ON THE EASTERN EMBANKMENT

Po Chü-i

	Transcription of Sound		Tone Pattern
Take money // buy flower trees	Chŕ chyán // mǎi hwā shù		− − ‖ + − +
Wall's east // on slope transplant	Chéng dūng // pō shàng dzāi	r	− − ‖ − + − r
Only purchase // have flower ones	Dàn gòu // yǒu hwā jě		+ + ‖ + − +
Not limit // peach apricot plum	Bú syàn // táu syìng méi	r	+ + ‖ − + − r
Hundred fruits // intermingle plant	Bǎi gwǒ // tsān dzá jùng		+ + ‖ − + +
Thousand branches // order sequence open	Chyān jr̄ // tsz̀ dì kāi	r	− − ‖ + + − r
Sky season // has early late	Tyān shŕ // yǒu dzǎu wǎn		− − ‖ + + +
Earth strength // hasn't high low	Dì lì // wú gāu dī	r	+ + ‖ − − − r
Red ones // rosy-vapor dazzling dazzling	Húng jě // syá yàn yàn		− + ‖ − + +
White ones // snow bright bright	Bái jě // sywě ái ái	r	+ + ‖ − − − r
Wandering bees // not leaving	Yóu fēng // jú bú chyù		− − ‖ + + +
Lovely birds // also come roost	Hǎu nyǎu // yì lái syī	r	+ + ‖ + − − r
Before have // long flowing waters	Chyán yǒu // cháng lyóu shwěi		− + ‖ − − +
Below have // small level terrace	Syà yǒu // syǎu píng tái	r	+ + ‖ + − − r
Sometimes brush // stones on terrace	Shŕ fú // tái shàng shŕ		− + ‖ − + +
Betimes raise // cup before wind	Yì jyǔ // fēng chyán bēi	r	+ + ‖ − − − r
Flower branch // shade my head	Hwā jr̄ // yìn wǒ tóu		− − ‖ + + −
Flower bud // drop-on my bosom	Hwā rwěi // lwò wǒ hwái	r	− + ‖ + + − r
Alone pour // again alone sing	Dú jwó // fù dú yǔng		+ + ‖ + + +
Not aware // sun level west	Bù jywé // r̀ píng syī	r	+ + ‖ + − − r
Pa custom // not love flowers	Bā sú // bú ài hwā		− + ‖ + + −
End spring // haven't person come	Jìng chwūn // wú rén lái	r	+ − ‖ − − − r
Only this // tipsy Great Protector	Wéi tsž // dzwèi Tài Shǒu		− + ‖ + + +
All day // not able-to return	Jìn r̀ // bù néng hwéi	r	+ + ‖ + − − r

東坡種花　　白居易

持錢買花樹
城東坡上栽
但購有花者
不限桃杏梅
百果參雜種
千枝次第開
天時有早晚
地力無高低
紅者霞豔豔
白者雪皚皚
遊蜂逐不去
好鳥亦棲來
前有長流水
下有小平臺
時拂臺上石
一舉風前杯
花枝蔭我頭
花蘂落我懷
獨酌復獨詠
不覺日平西
巴俗不愛花
竟春無人來
唯此醉太守
盡日不能迴

3

SONG OF COURTSHIP

FROM *The Book of Songs*

詩經

Transcription of Sound

[In] open-country are creeping plants	Yě yǒu màn tsǎo	
Falling dew plentiful Oh	Líng lù twán syī	a
There-is beautiful one person	Yǒu měi yì rén	
Clear broad-browed lovely Oh[1]	Chīng yáng wǎn syī	a
By chance encountering each-other met	Syè hòu syāng yù	
Fit my wishes Oh	Shr̀ wǒ ywàn syī	a
[In] open-country are creeping plants	Yě yǒu màn tsǎo	
Falling dew thick thick	Líng lù ráng ráng	b
There-is beautiful one person	Yǒu měi yì rén	
Lovely and clear broad-browed	Wǎn rú chīng yáng	b
By chance encountering each-other met	Syè hòu syāng yù	
With you together good[2]	Yǔ dž jyē dzāng	b

野有蔓草
零露漙兮
有美一人
清揚婉兮
邂逅相遇
適我願兮

野有蔓草
零露瀼瀼
有美一人
婉如清揚
邂逅相遇
與子偕臧

[1]Another interpretation would have it "Clear and bright of eye"
[2]Or "With you together hide away."

4.

A SUMMER DAY

Li Po

	Transcription of Sound		Tone Pattern
Lazy wave white feather fan	Lǎn yáu bái yǔ shàn		+ − + + +
Naked body in green forest	Lwǒ tǐ chīng lín jūng	r	+ + − − − r
Remove cap hang stone cliff	Twō jīn gwà shŕ bì		+ − + + +
Expose head sprinkle pine wind	Lù dǐng sǎ sūng fēng	r	+ + + − − r

山間夏日　李白

嬾搖白羽扇
躶體青林中
脫巾挂石壁
露頂灑松風

5.

THE SOLDIER'S SONG

FROM *The Book of Songs*

	Transcription of Sound	
What grass not yellow	Hé tsǎu bù hwáng	a
What day not march	Hé r̀ bù syíng	a
What man not go	Hé rén bù jyāng	a
Regulate manage four regions	Jīng yíng sz̀ fāng	a
What grass not dark	Hé tsǎu bù sywán	b
What man not ill	Hé rén bù gwān	b
Alas we expedition men	Āi wǒ jēng fū	
Alone are non-people	Dú wéi fěi mín	b
Not rhinoceroses not tigers	Fěi sz̀ fěi hǔ	c
Go-along empty wilds	Shwài bǐ kwàng yě	c
Alas we expedition men	Āi wǒ jēng fū	
Day night not at-leisure	Jāu syì bù syá	c
Thickly (-furred) fox	Yǒu péng jě hú	c
Goes-along these deep grasses	Shwài bǐ yōu tsǎu	d
Lofty carts	Yǒu jàn jr̄ jyū	c
March that Chou road	Syíng bǐ Jōu dàu	d

詩經

何草不黃
何日不行
何人不將
經營四方

何草不玄
何人不矜
哀我征夫
獨為匪民

匪兕匪虎
率彼曠野
哀我征夫
朝夕不暇

有芃者狐
率彼幽草
有棧之車
行彼周道

6.

TO HIM I LOVE

Tzu Yeh

	Transcription of Sound		Tone Pattern
Beloved sad // myself also pained	Hwān chóu // núng yì tsǎn		− − ‖ − + +
Sir smiles // I'm then happy	Láng syàu // wǒ byàn syǐ	r	− + ‖ + + + r
Don't see // joined annual-ring trees[1]	Bú jyàn // lyán lǐ shù		+ + ‖ − + +
Different roots // same branch rise	Yì gēn // túng tyáu chǐ	r	+ − ‖ − − + r

[1]Two trees whose trunks or branches have grown together.

贈愛　女子子夜

歡愁儂亦慘
郎笑我便喜
不見連理樹
異根同條起

7.

AT WEI RIVER FARM

Wang Wei

	Transcription of Sound		Tone Pattern
Slanting rays // shine-on market village	Syé gwāng // jàu syū lwò		− − ‖ + − +
Deep lane // cattle sheep return	Chyúng syàng // nyóu yáng gwēi	r	− + ‖ − − − r
Country elder // thinks-of shepherd boy	Yě lǎu // nyàn mù túng		+ + ‖ + + −
Leans-on staff // waits brushwood gate	Yǐ jàng // hòu jīng fēi	r	+ + ‖ + − − r
Pheasant cries // wheat shoots bloom	Jr̀ gòu // mài myáu syòu		+ + ‖ + − +
Silkworms sleep // mulberry leaves few	Tsán myán // sāng yè syī	r	− − ‖ − + − r
Field men // shoulder hoes stand	Tyán fū // hè chú lì		− − ‖ + − +
One-another see // speak lingering lingering	Syāng jyàn // yǔ yī yī	r	− + ‖ + − − r
Come here // envy leisure ease	Jí tsž // syàn syán yì		+ + ‖ + − +
Dejectedly // sing "Shih-wei"	Chàng rán // gē shr̀ wéi	r	+ − ‖ − + − r

渭川田家　　王維

斜光照墟落
窮巷牛羊歸
野老念牧童
倚杖候荊扉
雉雊麥苗秀

蠶眠桑葉稀
田夫荷鋤立
相見語依依
即此羨閒逸
悵然歌式微

8.

SONG OF THE WHITE CLOUDS

Ancient Source

	Transcription of Sound	
White cloud in the sky	Bái yún dzài tyān	
Hill mound self come out	Chyōu líng dz̀ chū	r
Road's miles distant far	Dàu lǐ yōu yuǎn	
Mountain river separate (us from) them	Shān chuān jyàn jr̄	r
Ask you not to die	Jyāng dž wú sž	
Wish again can come	Shàng fù néng lái	r

白雲謠

白雲在天
丘陵自出
道里悠遠
山川間之
將子無死
尚復能來

9.

WISE AGE TO YOUTH

Tu Ch'iu-niang

Urge you don't cherish // gold thread garment
Urge you should cherish // few years time[1]
Flowers open worthy pluck // straightaway should pluck
Don't wait no flowers // vainly pluck twigs

[1]Youth

Transcription of Sound

Chywàn jyūn mwò syí // jīn lyǔ yī	r
Chywàn jyūn syū syí // shào nyán shŕ	r
Hwā kāi kān jé // jŕ syū jé	
Mwò dài wú hwā // kūng jé jr̄	r

Tone Pattern

+	−	+	+	‖	−	+	−	r
+	−	−	+	‖	+	−	−	r
−	−	−	+	‖	+	−	+	
+	+	−	−	‖	−	+	−	r

金縷衣　　杜秋娘

勸君莫惜金縷衣
勸君須惜少年時
花開堪折直須折
莫待無花空折枝

10.

POEMS OF MY HEART

Juan Chi

	Transcription of Sound		Tone Pattern	
Open autumn // augur chilly wind	Kāi chyōu // jàu lyáng fēng		— — ‖ + — —	
Crickets cry // bed curtain	Syī shwài // míng chwáng wéi	r	+ + ‖ — — —	r
Moved-by things // hold-in-bosom great woe	Gǎn wù // hwái yīn yōu		+ + ‖ — — —	
Sadly sadly // makes heart grieve	Chyǎu chyǎu // lìng syīn bēi	r	+ + ‖ + — —	r
Many words // where place relate	Dwō yán // yān swǒ gàu		— — ‖ — + +	
Much talk // will tell whom	Fán tsź // jyāng sù shwéi	r	— — ‖ — + —	r
Slight wind // blows gauze sleeve	Wéi fēng // chwēi lwó mèi		— — ‖ — — +	
Bright moon // gleams clear radiance	Míng ywè // yàu chīng hwēi	r	— + ‖ + — —	r
Dawn chicken // cries tall tree	Chén jī // míng gāu shù		— — ‖ — — +	
Order harness-up // rise turn-back return	Mìng jyà // chǐ sywán gwēi	r	+ + ‖ + — —	r

詠懷詩　阮籍
第十四首

開秋兆涼風
蟋蟀鳴牀帷
感物懷殷憂
悄悄令心悲
多言焉所告
繁辭將訴誰
微風吹羅袂
明月耀清暉
晨雞鳴高樹
命駕起旋歸

11.

Excerpt from the description of the SHANG-LIN PARK OF THE SON OF HEAVEN

Ssu-ma Hsiang-ju

(translated by Burton Watson)

Behind them rise the tall mountains,
Lofty crests lifted to the sky;
Clothed in dense forests of giant trees,
Jagged with peaks and crags;
The steep summits of the Nine Pikes,
The towering heights of the Southern Mountains,
Soar dizzily like a stack of cooking pots,
Precipitous and sheer.
Their sides are furrowed with ravines and valleys,
Narrow-mouthed clefts and open glens,
Through which rivulets dart and wind.
About their base, hills and islands
Raise their tall heads;
Ragged knolls and hillocks
Rise and fall,
Twisting and twining
Like the coiled bodies of reptiles;
While from their folds the mountain streams leap and tumble,
Spilling out upon the level plains.
There they flow a thousand miles along smooth beds,
Their banks lined with dikes
Blanketed with green orchids
And hidden beneath selinea,
Mingled with snakemouth
And magnolias;
Planted with yucca,
Sedge of purple dye,
Bittersweet, gentians, and orchis,
Blue flag and crow-fans,
Ginger and tumeric,
Monkshood, wolfbane,
Nightshade, basil,
Mint, ramie, and blue artemisia,
Spreading across the wide swamps,
Rambling over the broad plains,
A vast and unbroken mass of flowers,
Nodding before the wind;
Breathing their fragrance,
Pungent and sweet,
A hundred perfumes
Wafted abroad
Upon the scented air.

Transcription of Sound

Yū shr̀ hū
Chúng shān chù chù a
Lúng dzūng tswēi wéi b
Shēn lín jyù mù a
Chán yán tsēn tsz̄ b
Jyǒu dzūng jyé yè
Nán shān é é b
Yán yí yǎn chí b
Tswēi wěi jywé chī b
Jèn syí tūng gǔ a
Jyǎn chǎn gōu dú a
Hān syā hwò yà c
Fù líng byé dǎu c
Wēi kwěi wěi hwēi b
Chyōu syū kū lěi b
Yǐn lín yù lěi b
Dēng jyàng shr̄ mǐ b
Pí chŕ bì chǎi b
Yěn rúng yín yù a
Sàn hwàn yí lù a
Tíng gāu chyān lǐ

Mǐ bù pī jú a
Yǎn yǐ lyù hwèi
Bèi yǐ jyāng lí b
Rǒu yí mí wú
Dzá yǐ lyóu yí b
Bù jyé lyǔ
Dzǎn lì swō b
Jyē chē héng lán d
Gǎu běn shè gān d
Dž jyāng ráng hé
Jēn chŕ rwò swūn d
Syān jr̄ hwáng lì
Jyǎng jù chīng fán d
Bù hwò húng dzé
Yán màn tài ywán d
Lí mí kwǎng yǎn
Yìng fēng pī mǐ e
Tù fāng yáng lyè
Yù yù fēi fēi
Jùng syāng fā ywè e
Syì syàng bù syě
Àn ài byé fú e

上林　　司馬相如

於是乎
崇山矗矗
巃嵷崔巍
深林巨木
嶄巖參嵳
九嵕巀嶭
南山峨峨
巖陁甗錡
摧崣崛崎
振溪通谷
蹇產溝瀆

谽呀豁閜
阜陵別隝
崴磈嵔廆
丘虛堀礨
隱轔鬱壘
登降施靡
陂池貏豸
沇溶淫鬻
散渙夷陸
亭皋千里
靡不被築

揜以綠蕙
被以江離
糅以蘼蕪
雜以留夷
布結縷
攢戾莎
揭車衡蘭
稾本射干
茈薑蘘荷
葴持若蓀
鮮支黃礫

蔣芧青薠
布濩閎澤
延曼太原
離靡廣衍
應風披靡
吐芳揚烈
郁郁菲菲
眾香發越
肸蠁布寫
晻薆咇茀

12.

LAMENT OF THE FARM WIFE OF WU

Su Tung-p'o

	Transcription of Sound		Tone Pattern	
This year rice paddy // ripens bitterly late	Jīn nyán gēng dàu // shú kǔ chŕ	a	− − − + ‖ + + −	a
Soon see frost wind // come how much time	Shù jyàn shwāng fēng // lái jǐ shŕ	a	+ + − − ‖ − + −	a
Wind frost come time // rain like outpouring	Fēng shwāng lái shŕ // yǔ rú syè		− − − − ‖ + − +	
Harrow head grows fungus // sickle sprouts coating	Pá tóu chū jyùn // lyán shēng yì	a	− − + + ‖ − − −	a
Eyes dry tears end // rain doesn't end	Yǎn kǔ lèi jìn // yǔ bú jìn		+ − + + ‖ + + +	
(How) bear see yellow ears // lie green mud	Rěn jyàn hwáng swèi // wò chīng ní	a	+ + − + ‖ + − −	a
Thatch cote one month // on embankment lodged	Máu shān yí ywè // lǔng shàng sù		− − + + ‖ + + +	
Sky clear harvest paddy // follow wagon return	Tyān chíng hwò dàu // swéi chē gwēi	a	− − + + ‖ + − −	a
Sweat flow shoulder red // transport enter market	Hàn lyóu jyān chēng // dzài rù shr̀		+ − − − ‖ + + +	
Price mean give away // like bran chaff	Jyà chyán chì yǔ // rú kāng syī	a	+ + + + ‖ − − −	a
Sell cow pay tax // split up roof cook	Mài nyóu nà shwèi // chāi wū chwēi	a	+ + + + ‖ + + −	a
Plan shallow doesn't reach // next year hunger	Lyù chyǎn bù jí // míng nyán jī	a	+ + + + ‖ − − −	a
Officials now want cash // don't want rice	Gwān jīn yàu chyán // bú yàu mǐ		− − + − ‖ + + +	
West north ten-thousand *li* // invite Tangut boys	Syī běi wàn lǐ // jāu Chyāng ér	a	− + + + ‖ − − −	a
Kung Huang fill court // people more suffer-bitterly	Gūng Hwáng mǎn cháu // rén gèng kǔ	b	− − + − ‖ − + +	b
I'd rather be // River Lord wife	Bù rú chywè dzwò // Hé Bwó fù	b	+ − + + ‖ − + +	b

吳中田婦歎　　蘇東坡

今年粳稻熟苦遲
庶見霜風來幾時
風霜來時雨如瀉
杷頭出菌鐮生衣
眼枯淚盡雨不盡
忍見黃穗臥青泥
茅苫一月隴上宿
天晴穫稻隨車歸
汗流肩赬載入市
價錢乞與如糠粞
賣牛納稅拆屋炊
慮淺不及明年飢
官今要錢不要米
西北萬里招羌兒
龔黃滿朝人更苦
不如却作河伯婦

13.

TO THE TUNE "SPRING OF WU-LING"

Li Ch'ing-chao

	Transcription of Sound		Tone Pattern	
Wind stops dust fragrant flowers already finished	Fēng jù chén syāng hwā yǐ jìn		− + − − − + +	
Day late tiredly comb hair	R̀ wǎn jywàn shū tóu	r	+ + + − −	r
Objects are man is-not things cease	Wù shr̀ rén fēi shr̀ shr̀ syōu	r	+ + − − + + −	r
Want-to speak tears first flow	Yù yǔ lèi syān lyóu	r	+ + + − −	r
Hear say Twin Streams spring still fine	Wén shuō Shwāng Syī chwūn shàng hǎu		− + − − − + +	
Also will float light boat	Yě nǐ fàn chīng jōu	r	+ + + − −	r
Only fear Twin Streams "locust-skiff" boat	Jř kǔng Shwāng Syī dzé měng jōu	r	+ + − − + + −	r
Can not bear so much sorrow	Dzài bú dùng syǔ dwō chóu	r	+ + + + − −	r

武陵春　李清照

風住塵香花已盡
日晚倦梳頭
物是人非事事休
欲語淚先流

聞說雙溪春尚好
也擬泛輕舟
只恐雙溪舴艋舟
載不動許多愁

14.

DROUGHT

FROM *The Confucian Odes (No.258)*

	Transcription of Sound	
Drought already too severe	Hàn jì tài shèn	
Sultry heavy steamy steamy	Yùn lúng chúng chúng	a
Not cease pure-sacrifice offering	Bù tyǎn yīn sż	
From outland go-to hall	Dż jyāu tsú gūng	a
Above below[1] set bury	Shàng syà dyàn yì	
No spirit not honored	Mǐ shén bù dzūng	a
Hou chi not concerned	Hòu Jì bú kè	
God above doesn't approach	Shàng Dì bù lín	a
Destroy ruin earth below	Hàu dù syà tǔ	
Then light-on my person	Níng dīng wǒ gūng	a
Drought already too severe	Hàn jì tài shèn	
Bare bare mountains rivers	Dí dí shān chwān	b
Drought demon is cruel	Hàn bá wéi nywè	
As-if flaring as-if burning	Rú tán rú fén	b
Our minds fear heat	Wǒ syīn dàn shǔ	
Grieved minds as-if afire	Yōu syīn rú syūn	b
Many lords former rulers	Chyún gūng syān jèng	
Thereupon hear us not	Dzé bù wǒ wén	b
Great Heaven God Above	Hàn Tyān Shàng Dì	
Then let me escape	Níng bì wǒ dwùn	b

[1]i.e., sacrificing to heaven and earth.

詩經

旱既大甚
蘊隆蟲蟲
不殄禋祀
自郊徂宮
上下奠瘞
靡神不宗
后稷不克
上帝不臨
耗斁下土
寧丁我躬

旱既大甚
滌滌山川
旱魃為虐
如惔如焚
我心憚暑
憂心如熏
群公先正
則不我聞
昊天上帝
寧俾我遯

15.

Excerpt from LI SAO

Attributed to Ch'ü Yüan

(The characteristic prosodic unit of this poem is a line of three beats, an unstressed syllable, two beats, and the carrier-sound *syi,* followed by a line of three beats, the unstressed syllable, and two beats with rhyme. I have marked the unstressed syllables with parentheses.)

	Transcription of Sound	
Morning release brake (in) Ts'ang-wu oh	Jāu fā rèn (yú) Tsāng wú syī	a
Evening I arrive (at) Hsuan-p'u	Syì yú jr̀ (hū) Syàn pǔ	
Want awhile stay (this) spirit precinct oh	Yù shǎu lyóu (tsž) líng swǒ syī	a
Sun hasty hasty (so) will set	R̀ hū hū (chí) jyāng mù	a
I order Hsi-ho hold control oh	Wú lìng Syī hé mǐ jyé syī	
Gaze Yen-tzu (and) don't approach	Wàng Yān dz̄ (ér) wù pwò	a
Road far far (so) long distant oh	Lù màn màn (chí) syōu ywǎn syī	
I will go up go down (and) search delve	Wú jyāng shàng syà (ér) chyóu swǒ	a
I order *feng* bird fly upleap oh	Wú lìng fèng nyǎu fēi téng syī	
Continue it (by) days nights	Jì jr̄ (yǐ) r̀ yè	b
Whirling winds gather (so) attach to (me) oh	Pyāu fēng twún (chí) syāng lí syī	
Leading clouds rainbows (and) come great	Shwài yún ní (ér) lái yà	b
Extravagantly throng throng (so) part meet oh	Fēn dzǔng dzǔng (chí) lí hé syī	
Rich profusion confusion (so) go up go down	Bān lù lí (chí) shàng syà	b
I order God's gatekeeper open bolt oh	Wú lìng dì hwūn kāi gwān syī	
Lean Heaven's Gate and gaze me	Yǐ chāng hé (ér) wàng yú	b

離騷　屈原

朝發軔於蒼梧兮
夕余至乎縣圃
欲少留此靈瑣兮
日忽忽其將暮
吾令羲和弭節兮
望崦嵫而勿迫
路曼曼其修遠兮
吾將上下而求索

吾令鳳鳥飛騰兮
繼之以日夜
飄風屯其相離兮
帥雲霓而來御
紛總總其離合兮
斑陸離其上下
吾令帝閽開關兮
倚閶闔而望余

16.

LIGHT VERSE ON A ROCK

Wang Wei

	Transcription of Sound		Tone Pattern
Cherish-able huge rock // by fountain stream	Kě lyán pán shŕ // lín chywán shwěi		+ − − + ‖ − − +
Again have hanging willow // brush wine cup	Fù yǒu chwéi yáng // fú jyǒu bēi	r	+ + − − ‖ + + − r
How say spring wind // doesn't understand thoughts	Rwò dàu chwūn fēng // bù jyě yì		+ + − − ‖ + + +
What reason blow send // falling flowers come	Hé yīn chwēi sùng // lwò hwā lái	r	− − − + ‖ + − − r

戲題磐石　　王維

可憐磐石臨泉水
復有垂楊拂酒盃
若道春風不解意
何因吹送落花來

Bibliography

	Poem	Source
1.	South Wind	Tu-Fu (712-770) Rexroth, Kenneth, ed. & tr.: *One Hundred Poems from the Chinese* (New York: New Directions, 1971), p. 24.
2.	Planting Flowers on the Eastern Embankment	Po Chü-i (772-846) Waley, Arthur, ed. & tr.: *Translations from the Chinese,* 2d ed. (New York: Alfred A. Knopf, Inc., 1941), p. 216.
3.	Song of Courtship	(Probably compiled during the 7th century B.C.) Waley, Arthur, ed. & tr.: *The Book of Songs,* 2d ed. (New York: Grove Press Inc., 1960), p. 21.
4.	A Summer Day	Li Po (701-762) Obata, Shigeyoshi, ed. & tr.: *Works of Li Po, The Chinese Poet* (New York: Paragon Book Reprint Corp., 1965), p. 29.
5.	The Soldier's Song	(Probably compiled during the 7th century B.C.) Waley, Arthur, ed. & tr.: *The Book of Songs,* 2d ed. (New York: Grove Press Inc., 1960), p. 121.
6.	To Him I Love	Tzu Yeh (Chin Dynasty 265-419) Hart, Henry H., ed. & tr.: *Poems of the Hundred Names,* 4th ed. (New York: Greenwood Press, 1968), p. 55.

7.	At Wei River Farm	Wang Wei (701-761) Yin-nan, Chang and Walmsley, Lewis C., ed. & tr.: *Poems by Wang Wei* (Rutland, Vermont and Tokyo, Japan: Charles E. Tuttle Company, 1958), p. 130.
8.	Song of the White Clouds	From an ancient source (c. 1120 B.C.) Waddell, Helen, ed. & tr.: *Lyrics from the Chinese* (Boston: Houghton Mifflin Co., 1913), p. 40.
9.	Wise Age to Youth	Tu Ch'iu-niang (T'ang Dynasty 618-905) Hart, Henry H., ed. & tr.: *Poems of the Hundred Names,* 4th ed. (New York: Greenwood Press, 1968), p. 122.
10.	Poems of My Heart	Juan Chi (220-264) Ch'en, Jerome and Bullock, Michael, ed. & tr.: *Poems of Solitude* (Rutland, Vermont and Tokyo, Japan: Charles E. Tuttle Company, 1960), p. 15.
11.	Excerpt from the description of the Shang-lin Park of the Son of Heaven	Ssu-ma Hsiang-ju (c. 100 B.C.) Watson, Burton, tr. and De Bary, Wm. Theodore, ed.: *Early Chinese Literature* (New York and London: Columbia University Press, 1962), p. 276.
12.	Lament of the Farm Wife of Wu	Su Tung-p'o (1037-1101) Watson, Burton, ed. & tr.: *Su Tung-P'o: Selections from a Sung Dynasty Poet* (New York: Columbia University Press, 1965), p. 40.

13. To the Tune "Spring of Wu Ling"	Li Ch'ing-chao (1084-1142) Rexroth, Kenneth, ed. & tr.: *Love and the Turning Year: One Hundred More Poems from the Chinese* (New York: New Directions, 1970), p. 94.
14. Drought	(Probably compiled during the 7th century B.C.) Pound, Ezra, ed. & tr.: *The Confucian Odes: The Classic Anthology Defined by Confucius* (New York: New Directions, 1959), pp. 182, 183.
15. Excerpt from Li Sao	Attributed to Ch'ü Yüan (early 3d century B.C.). Hawkes, David, ed. & tr.: *Ch'u Tzu: The Songs of the South, An Ancient Chinese Anthology* (Boston: Beacon Press, 1962), pp. 28, 29.
16. Light Verse on a Rock	Wang Wei (701-761) Yin-nan, Chang and Walmsley, Lewis C., ed. & tr.: *Poems by Wang Wei* (Rutland, Vermont and Tokyo, Japan: Charles E. Tuttle Company, 1958), p. 77.

Biographies of Contributing Artists

SALLY F. NICHOLS — drawings
Sally Freeman Nichols was born in Boston. She has studied, worked and shown in the United States and Europe. In 1950, she was one of "Ten American Painters Living in Europe" exhibited in major Italian cities by the Italian Government. In 1969 her drawings were shown in various cities in England under the sponsorship of the Italian Embassy. She has paintings in private collections in Oslo, London, Cairo, Athens and Italy, as well as in the United States. She now lives with her husband, Elliott S. Nichols, in Kent, Connecticut. She is the mother of three children.

LORETTA PAN — Chinese calligraphy
Miss Loretta Pan, Senior Lecturer in Chinese at Columbia University and concurrently Adjunct Assistant Professor at Herbert H. Lehman College (CUNY) in the Bronx, came to this country in 1951 and did graduate work in English Literature at Mount Holyoke College in Massachusetts. In China she taught English and Chinese and served as Chief Translator at the British Embassy Information Department in China during the Second World War and as Chinese Editor at the American Consulate General in Hong Kong. She joined Columbia University in 1955 as Editorial Assistant on the project *Men and Politics in Modern China.* She started teaching Chinese at Columbia in 1960 and has been totally committed to excellence in her teaching during the past decade and a half following the tradition of the University. She compares herself to a fish whose water is Excellence. Her students have, with great enthusiasm and effort, kept her in her water through the years and won her great admiration. While she lives in the success of

her students, she strives constantly for self-improvement. The nine titles which she developed as teaching aids have been used at Columbia and Lehman and, upon request, in the Chinese language programs of several other universities in the U.S.A., Canada, and Australia.

STUART H. SARGENT — translations and analyses of poems
Stuart H. Sargent, a native of Oregon, has spent over three years in Asia — two in Japan and one in Taiwan — studying and teaching. He has also taught at the University of Hawaii. He is presently writing his dissertation in the field of Chinese poetry at Stanford University. Several poems translated by Mr. Sargent have appeared in *Renditions,* a translation journal published at the Chinese University of Hong Kong.

JEANYEE WONG — calligraphy for translations
Jeanyee Wong was born in San Francisco and started to study Chinese at the age of three. Her formal art training began at the Cooper Union in New York, where she studied painting, sculpture, lettering and design. Later, she apprenticed herself to Fritz Kredel to learn woodcutting and other illustration techniques. As a freelance calligrapher, designer and illustrator, she has done book jackets, greeting cards (including one for UNICEF), maps, letterheads and advertisements. She has illustrated or decorated many books, including a collection of Oriental fairy tales compiled by Pearl Buck.